Boudicca: The Flame-Haired Warrior Queen

By

D.M. Alon

Boudicca: The Flame-Haired Warrior Queen

Copyright © 2014 by D.M. Alon

Published and distributed by: Numinosity Press Incorporated.

Alon, Doron .

ISBN: 978-0692593981

Boudicca: The Flame-Haired Warrior Queen
–1st ed

Printed in the United States of America
doron@numinositypress.com

Images used for Cover and content:
Cover Created by Shahnaz Mohammed
mailto:NAZNYC@GMAIL.COM
Alexander the Great © v0v - Fotolia.com
Joan Of Arc © Tupungato - Fotolia.com
Ghnegis Kahn © Andrey Burmakin - Fotolia.com
Akhenaten © Travis Hiner - Fotolia.com

http://www.amazon.com/author/dmalon

Dedication
Dedicated to the Heroic Spirit of Boudicca

Introduction

As the Roman Empire swept through Europe, it conquered almost all the lands it came across. It became the most hated empire the world had ever known. Despite their great success at subjecting the known world, they did not achieve these victories without a fight. Throughout their conquests, they met with fierce resistance. These various resistance movements culminated in numerous wars. Some wars lasting for several bloody years and some, not so long. It took a special person to even dare defy Roman Rule.

One of these special people was Boudicca, (Often spelled Boudica or Boudicea) ,born around A.D 25 to a Royal family of the Briton tribe of Iceni, in Celtic Britain. Not very much is known about her life, much of it remains somewhat of a mystery. The little information we have comes from two prominent historians; Cassius Dio (A.D. 150-235) and Publius Cornealius Tacitus (A.D 56-117).

From what we can glean from these two men about Boudicca is fascinating. When Rome humiliated her and her people. She, in her righteous anger faced Rome head-on; rallying her people against them. In many ways, she is one of the great heroines of history.

In this book, we will discuss, ever so briefly, Boudicca, The Flame-Haired Warrior Queen.

The Roman Conquest of Britannia

In order to understand Boudicca's life, and her prominence in history, we will briefly venture into the history of Britannia (Modern day Britain)as it relates to Rome. This is vital. In order to understand who she was, we must understand why she became who she became. The only way to do this is to go back a bit in time.

The famed general and future dictator, Gaius Julius Caesar entered Britannia during his conquest of Gaul (Modern Day France), for the first time between 55 and 54 BC, nearly 80 years before Boudicca was born. His goal, of course, was conquest. During this time, several tribes offered to be allies of the Romans. One of these tribes was the Iceni, the tribe in which Boudicca would be the future Queen. Caesar, however, had some difficulties. Not all Briton Tribes were quite so inviting and this caused him to experience serious military hardships. In addition, the seas surrounding Britannia were very difficult to navigate. After securing his tribute from the friendly Briton tribes, Julius left, never to return to Britannia again. In fact, the Roman army did not return to Britannia for nearly 100 years.

However, the Romans still traded with the Britons in the south east via Gaul. The Iceni, who were in the east, did not participate in that rich trade, but that did not mean they were not wealthy. Their Southern neighbors, mainly the Catuvellauni were the beneficiaries of such trade. They imported cattle, metals, pottery, grain and gold coins and other valuable items. In short, the Catuvellauni were becoming very wealthy.

The grain that was imported from Britannia was very important for the ever growing Roman Empire. They knew that any country that had a lot of grain needed to be added to the fold. This is what they would do to Egypt .

Emperor Claudius

Fast forward to 41 A.D ,the Roman Empire had a new Emperor, Claudius aka Tiberius Claudius Augustus Germanicus, replacing his blood thirsty nephew Caligula who was assassinated that same year. During Claudius's early reign, things were getting a bit hectic in Britannia and Gaul. Rumor had it that the Britons were the ones causing the unrest. Although there was unrest, it was not a huge problem just yet. However, Claudius wanted to launch a military offensive anyway.

Some questioned his motives. He was not exactly the example of physical strength and vigor. He was known to stutter, and to be partially deaf due to a childhood illness. In addition, he suffered from a limp. (As an aside, these apparent short comings most probably turned out to be his saving grace. His family was notorious for killing one another. His disabilities most likely saved him). BUT at the same time, he was made to feel inadequate, so a winning military campaign in Gaul and Britannia would boost his rather frail image. He decided to Invade in 43 AD.

When the Romans landed in Britannia right at the southeastern coast, they found that several tribes welcomed the invasion, but the tribe, the Iceni, from which Boudicca was from did not, nor did their very rich neighbor , the Catuvellauni. The Iceni was ruled by Antedios at the time. The King of the Catuvellauni known to the Romans as Caractacus and his brother Togodumnus attempted do raise a rebellion against the Romans.

Once on the ground, the allied forces led by Caractacus attacked the Romans. This was not very successful, they eventually ended up retreating. At this time, Caractacuss' brother was killed and the Romans won this major initial battle. Claudius, upon hearing of his victory arrived at Britannia and accepted the surrender of various British rulers. One ruler being Antedios , the ruler of Iceni. Boudicca, was 18 years old when this occurred. She was most aware of what was going on.

After this victory, the Britons were hoping the Romans would take what they needed to take and leave them alone as Julius Caesar did. They were sorely mistaken. Instead of leaving, the Romans hunkered down and entrenched their position. Claudius built a fortress at Camulodunum the capital for a tribe called the Trinovantes who were just south of the Iceni and east of the Catuvellauni. Other fortresses were also built. He appointed Aulus Plautius as the very first Roman Governor in Britannia. Despite this, the king of Catuvellauni did not give up entirely. He was secretly amassing more forces and menaced the Romans every chance he had.

In 47 AD, Aulus Plautius was replaced by Ostorius Scapula. During this transition of power, the rebel force led by Caractacus raided. This did not amuse Scapula. He eventually ordered the disarmament of the tribes the Romans had put under their control. It appeared that he lost trust in all Briton tribes, not just the ones that were avowed enemies of Rome. Little did he know, they were secretly stockpiling weapons. This disarmament angered the Iceni which attempted a rebellion of their own. This was unsuccessful, Scapula easily defeated them and replaced Antedios with a man named Prasutagas , who became the new king of the Iceni.

Boudicca's Humiliation

Prasutagas was married to Boudicca. Thus making her Queen of the Iceni. Boudicca, as I mentioned in the introduction is very much a mystery. We do know that she was born to a Royal family around AD 25. This seems to be the consensus of historians Dio and Tacitus.

Dio went on further to describe Boudicca as "possessed of greater intelligence than often belongs to women". This betrays the misogyny of the day. She was also thought to be rather tall and having bright fiery red hair. Dio goes on to say that she had a soul piercing stare and a harsh voice. She also appeared to practice the ancient Druidic religion of the Celts.

Her husband, Prasutagas, was very rich and lived quite the life. He was very eager to maintain his lineage so he made his wife Boudicca and their 2 daughters co-heirs to his kingdom. He also appointed Scapula as co-heir as well. That seems like a rather odd thing to do. However, it was common Roman practice. The practice essentially allows client kings independence for as long as they lived and forced them to agree to leave their respective kingdoms to Rome upon their passing.

When Prasutagas died in 60 AD, Rome (who had a new emperor, emperor Nero) ignored his request to make his wife and children co-heirs and took over his territory. This may seem unfair, but according to Roman law, inheritance can only pass through the male. This meant that only Scapula had any real claim to Prasutagas's property. Prasutagas property was seized and some of the inhabitants were made slaves of the empire. This turn of events left Boudicca and her daughters out in the cold. But that was not all.

Boudicca fought this unfair seizer but that only inspired Rome's wrath. Boudicca and her daughters were to suffer horrible indignities due to their insolence. Boudicca was flogged and her daughters were brutally raped. To add insult to injury, it turned out Prasutagas in his profligacy owed Rome an enormous amount of money. The Romans were now calling in those loans. His subjects were on the hook for this now. Rome was ruthless in their collection of these debts; seizing property and using brute force at every opportunity.

A year later , AD 61, to add even further fuel to the fire, Caius Suetonius Paulinus the new governor of Britannia who replaced Scapula was on a military campaign. He started his reign with one. He reached the Isle of Mona, a Briton stronghold and holy site. What the Romans saw there was unlike anything they have ever seen, it in essence froze the Romans stiff when they encountered this.Among the heavily armed masses were women in black robes carrying torches while looking frightfully disheveled. Amongst the crowd were also priests of the druid religion pronouncing curses at the Romans. Despite this scene, however, Caius Suetonius Paulinus ordered his men to not fear these people and proceeded with the campaign, eventually ending in a Roman Victory.

Once the Isle of Mona was under control, Caius Suetonius Paulinus started to dismantle sacred sites the Druids held dear. Many of these sites were used for ritual sacrifice. At this point, Boudicca had had enough. It was time to rid themselves of the Latin Menace.

Boudicca - The Flame-Haired Warrior Queen

Now, inflamed with righteous anger, Boudicca had enough as did many of the tribes. The desecration of the Isle of Mona was just too much. On top of that, Boudicca wanted revenge for what she and her daughters personally endured at the hands of the Romans.

Having acquired many weapons after secretly stockpiling them as I mentioned earlier, they had enough to mount a significant attack against the Romans. Boudicca, after consulting an oracle decided it was now time to mount a serious rebellion.

Boudicca moved quickly against a Roman Colony at Camulodnum, which the Romans seized from the Trinovantes. After the Romans seized Camulodnum they did not fortify it thinking the Britons were really no threat. This, however was a grave error. It was said that throughout Camulodnum, horrible doom-filled shrieks would pierce through the air and that the sea turned blood red and that the ebb and flow of the tide resembled dead bodies. These signs were viewed by the Britons as fortuitous.

Boudicca easily took Camulodnum back from the Romans and the Roman army quickly fled to a temple. A few days later, the temple fell. At this point, the Romans did not have adequate backup. The only force that was available was the Legion IX Hispania. They were not very well manned but they had no time to lose. They rushed to assist but never arrived to Camulodnum. She made sure they would never make it. She killed the infantry. The Legion IX Hispanias commander Quintus Petilius Cerialis Caesius Rufus, with his cavalry took cover in Londinium (Modern day London).

There was one hope for the Romans though. Caius Suetonius Paulinus was still available. He was finishing up his business in the Isle of Mona. When he heard Boudicca led a rebellion he rushed to assist, but Londinium was very hard to defend, it was too large and not well fortified by the Romans. Caius Suetonius Paulinus realized that Londinium was a lost cause and let it fall to Boudicca.

And fall it did, Boudicca made sure that every Roman she found there was killed. According to some historians, the brutality of her army was unprecedented. According to Dio they took noble women, hung them up naked and cut off their breasts and worse, they had the breasts sown to their mouths making them look they were eating them. Then to finish them off, they would impale the women lengthwise. Accounts like these do need to be taken with some caution. It is not uncommon for historians to embellish these kinds of brutal acts. Especially if the subject of their work is considered an enemy.

Despite letting Londinium go, he wasn't about to surrender himself. Caius Suetonius Paulinus had about 10,000 soldiers from the 15th legion and some from the 20th legion. He also had access to Legion 2 and called for their support.

Suetonius chose a position with a wooded forest to his rear. He chose this location since he knew Boudicca's army of 230,000 strong would attack from open spaces as opposed to the forest. He felt safe. Despite being outnumbered, Suetonius knew that the Romans had a higher caliber of training than the Britons and that gave them an advantage. The Romans have proven time and time again that although outnumbered, proper and adequate training made all the difference. The Britons knew they outnumbered the Romans and this made them cocky. If history is any indication, cockiness is deadly on the battlefield. One display of this hubris was the fact that the men brought their wives with them so they could witness their upcoming victory. Even Boudicca decided to bring her daughters along as well.

The Romans were ready for battle. However, they still needed some boost to their morale. They were frightened by the unconventional Briton forces. Suetonius encouraged the army telling them that most of the fighting force were not men at arms and those who were present were not very well armed or trained and could be easily defeated.

The Romans were far more well equipped. They had chariots for the open fields. They had solid shields and a short sword that allowed them brutal efficiency at close range without losing speed. The Britons used a longer sword which inhibited their movements substantially. Unlike a short sword, a long sword needs more space to wield. This would prove quite disastrous for Boudicca's army. It slowed them down.

Despite Boudicca's numbers, the Roman advantages above proved to be the deciding factor. The Romans truly defeated the Britons, killing men, women and children. Many animals were also slaughtered. According to Tacitus up to 80,000 Britons were killed but only 400 Romans.

Although Boudicca's initial attempt at rebellion succeeded, it was clear at this point the overall rebellion had failed miserably. It was said at this point that Boudicca, fearing capture committed suicide, while others say she died of wounds she sustained on the battle field. Although Boudicca was dead, the Romans continued their campaign against the Britons and effectively crushed them.

The Flame Has Been Extinguished

Boudicca was dead. Her people were deeply grieved. They gave her the most lavish burial they could afford. Her people effectively crushed. But her legend carried on in their hearts. Ironically, her vision of justice and peace did come to fruition, albeit under Roman Rule. Britannia became a fully participating territory within the Roman Empire. Rome did not want another rebellion so they instituted Just laws and a structure that brought peace to the region. Boudicca , in death, was victorious after all. But her true vision of a Rome-free Britain would only come in 410 A.D when the Goths of the East overtook the Romans. The Romans fled from Britain, never to return.

About The Interviews With History Series

The goal of the Interviews With History series is to provide concise biographical information for people who want to read biographies, but do not have the time to read hundreds of pages or purchase expensive study courses. What you read in an Interviews With History Titles are the pertinent facts; no filler. Written in an easy to understand and conversational fashion. To learn about future releases in this series please visit www.amazon.com/author/dmalon

Other Books In The Interviews With History Series

ABOUT THE AUTHOR

D.M. Alon is a bestselling author of 50 books, in 5 different genres and founder of Numinosity Press Inc. He writes on a wide variety of topics. His conversational writing style and his ability to convert the esoteric into the mundane is his specialty; this has gained him popularity in the genres that he writes for.

Amazon Author Page: www.amazon.com/author/dmalon

Bibliography

Boudica: The British Revolt Against Rome AD 60

Boudica: Iron Age Warrior Queen

Boudica's Last Stand: Britain's Revolt Against Rome AD 60–61

One More Thing

If you liked this book, I would love for you to review it. Reviews are an authors bread and butter.

Thanks in advance.

www.ingramcontent.com/pod-product-compliance
Lightning Source LLC
Chambersburg PA
CBHW060551030426
42337CB00021B/4529